Celebrated Christma

6 Christmas Favorites Arranged for Intermediate to Late Intermediate Pianists

Robert D. Vandall

Christmas duets allow students to experience the joy of sharing music with a partner during the holiday season. The carols and songs chosen for the *Celebrated Christmas Duets* series are those most favored by students, as they love playing carols and songs that they know well. In these arrangements, both primo and secondo are crafted to be of equal difficulty and interest. Melodies are shared or passed between performers allowing students to benefit from the careful listening required to perform piano duets musically. In addition, I've used refreshing harmonies and unexpected rhythms, and added short introductions and codas to create satisfying musical experiences. The music itself truly captures the Christmas season.

Merry Christmas!

Contents

Alfred

Alfred Music Publishing Co., Inc.
P.O. Box 10003
Van Nuys, CA 91410-0003
alfred.com

ISBN-10: 0-7390-7356-7
ISBN-13: 978-0-7390-7356-8

The Hallelujah Chorus

SECONDO

George Frideric Handel
Arr. Robert D. Vandall

The Hallelujah Chorus

PRIMO

George Frideric Handel
Arr. Robert D. Vandall

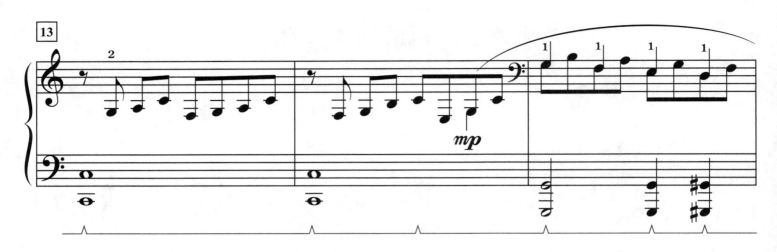

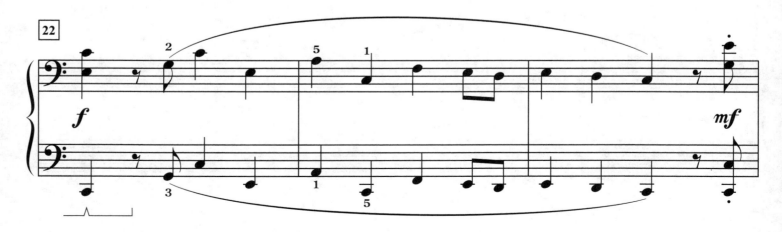

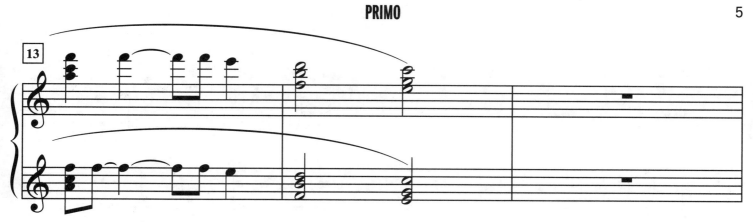

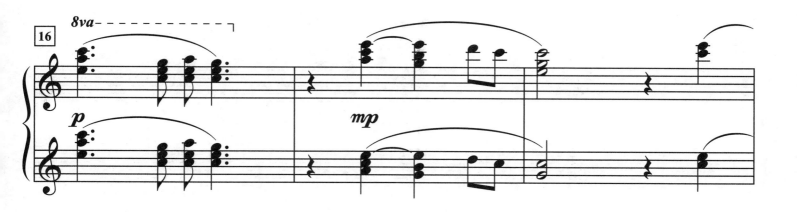

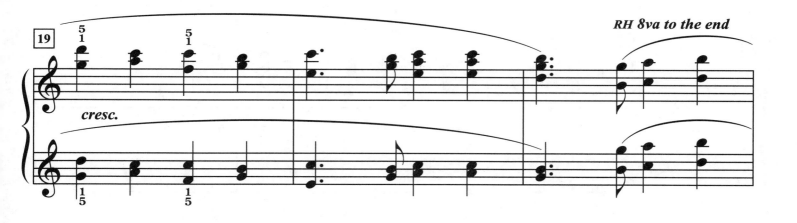

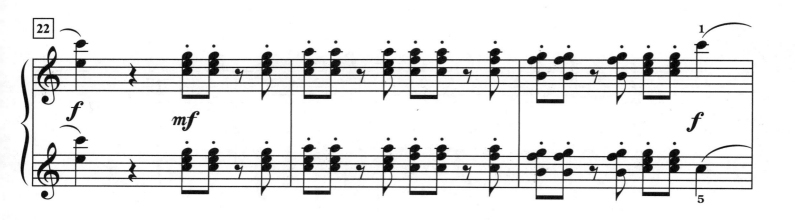

25

28

31

34

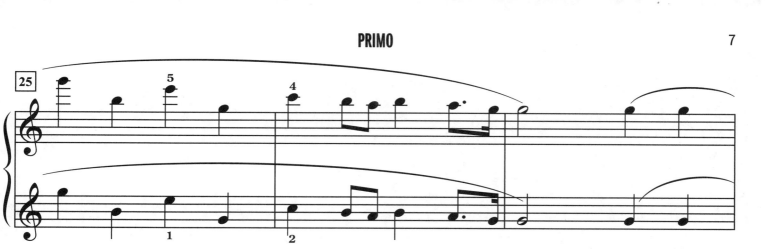

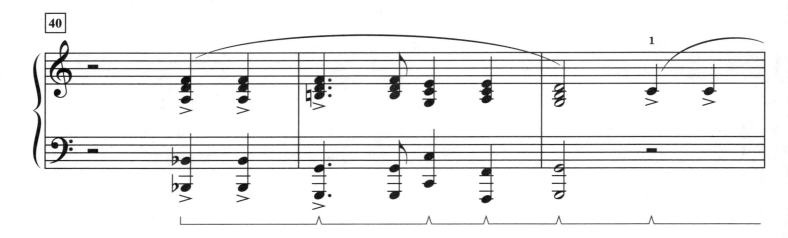

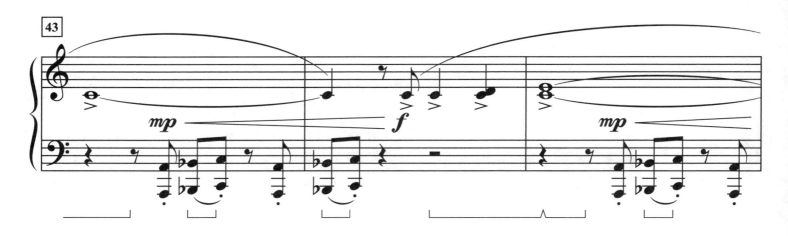

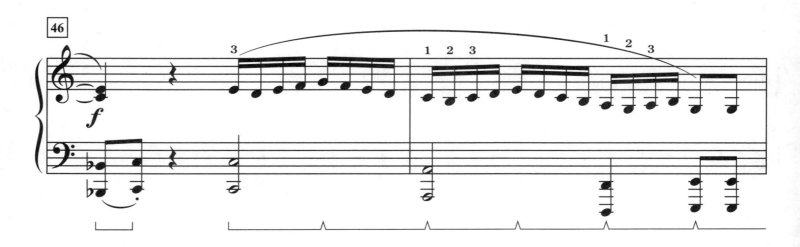

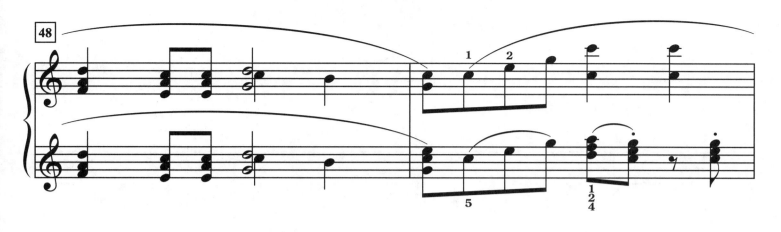

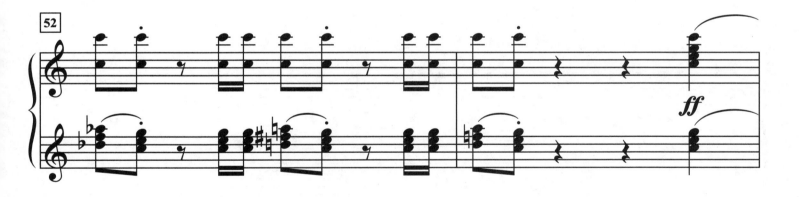

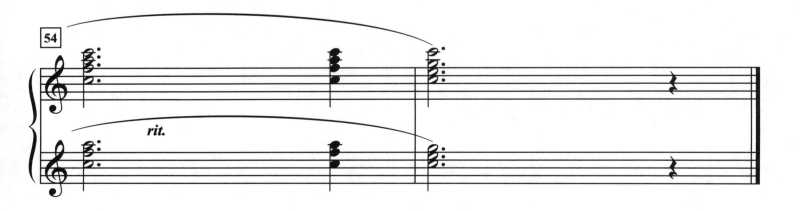

O Come, All Ye Faithful

SECONDO

John F. Wade
Arr. Robert D. Vandall

O Come, All Ye Faithful

PRIMO

John F. Wade
Arr. Robert D. Vandall

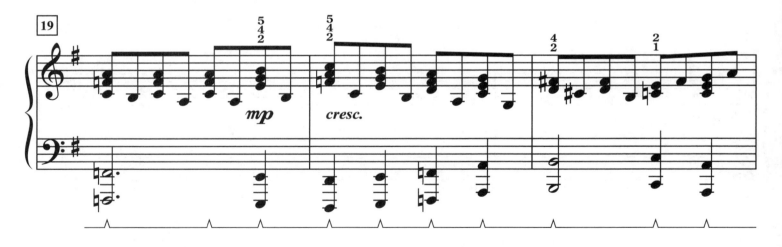

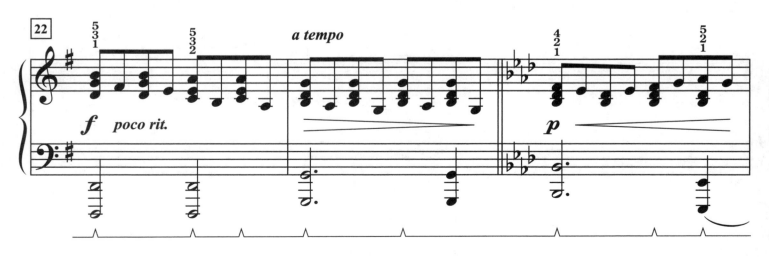

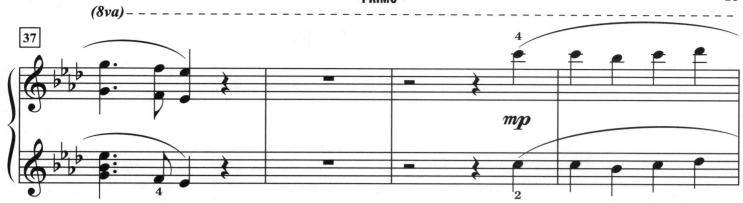

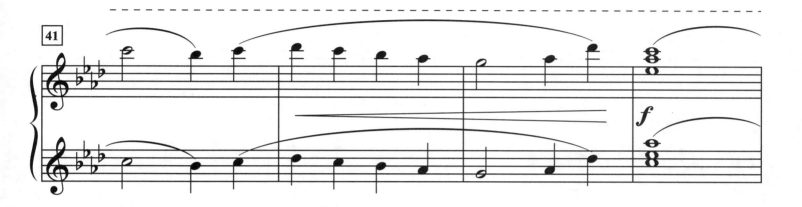

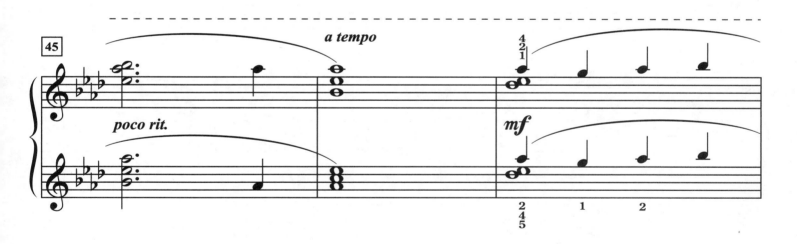

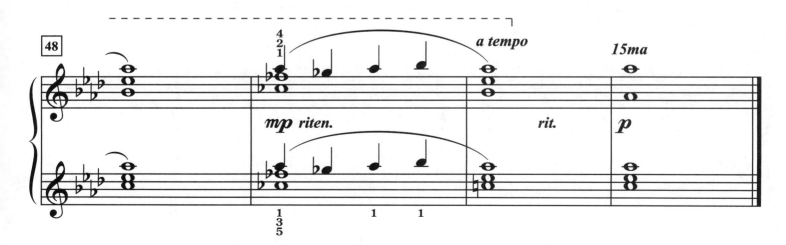

Deck the Halls

SECONDO

Welsh Carol
Arr. Robert D. Vandall

Deck the Halls

PRIMO

Welsh Carol
Arr. Robert D. Vandall

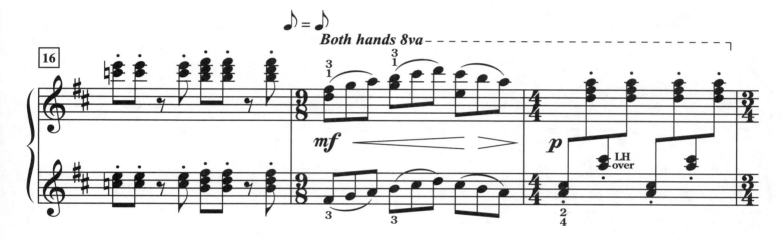

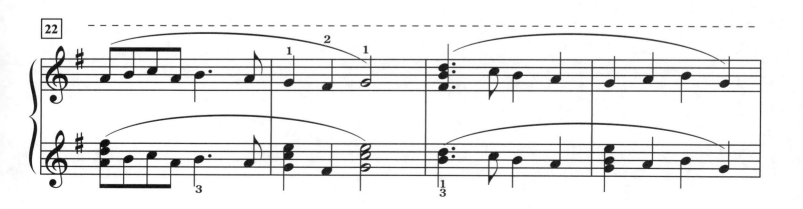

SECONDO

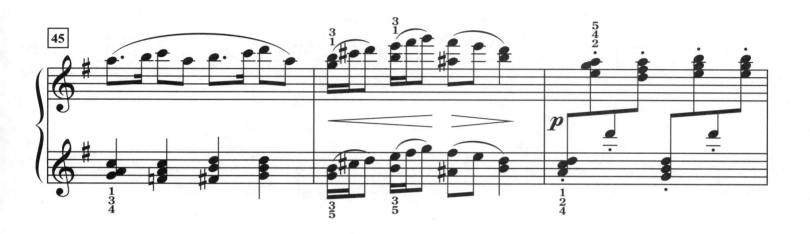

Silent Night

SECONDO

Franz Grüber
Arr. Robert D. Vandall

Silent Night

PRIMO

Franz Grüber
Arr. Robert D. Vandall

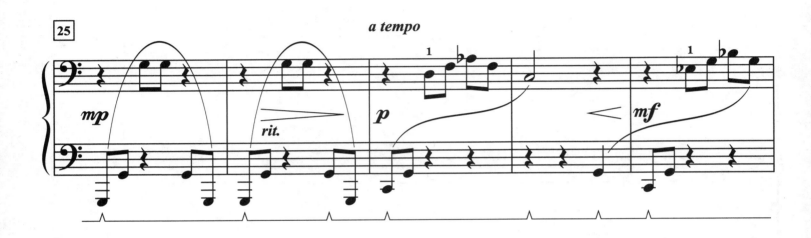

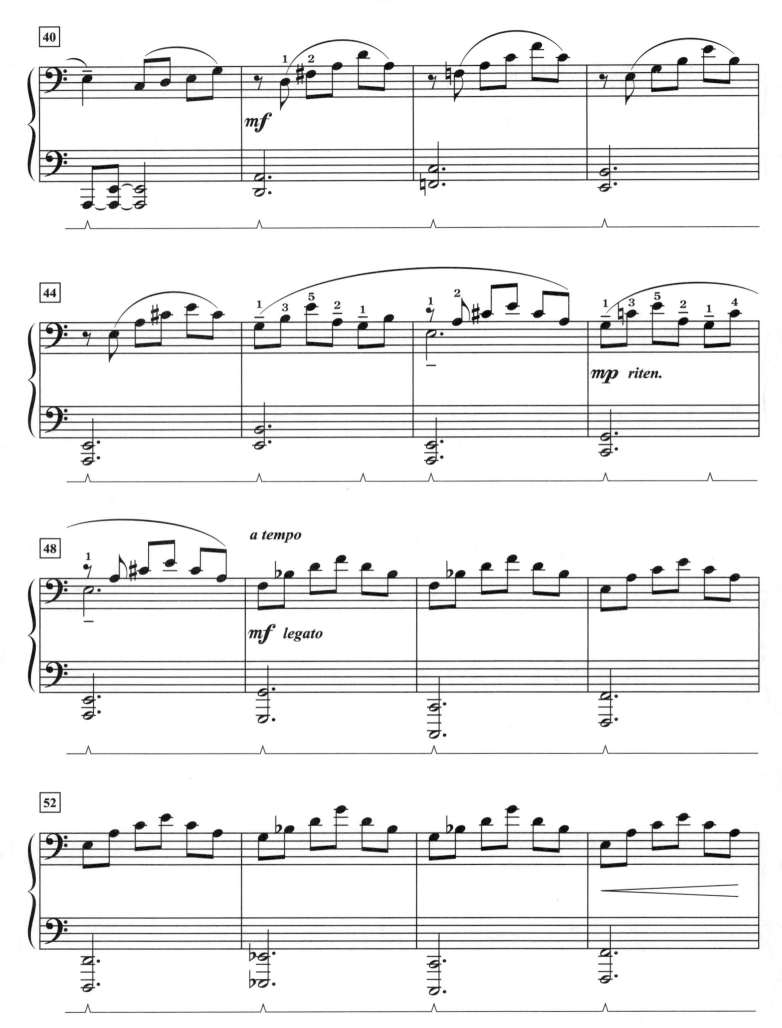

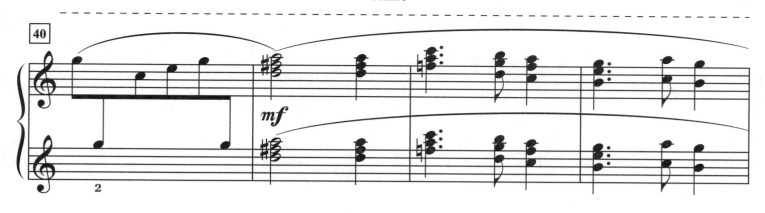

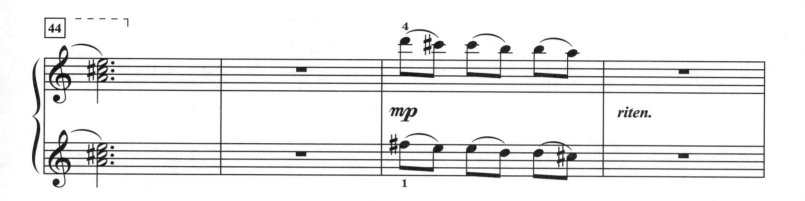

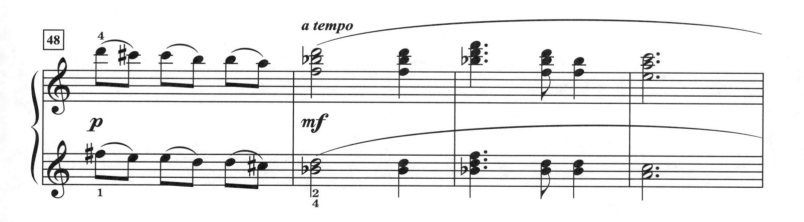

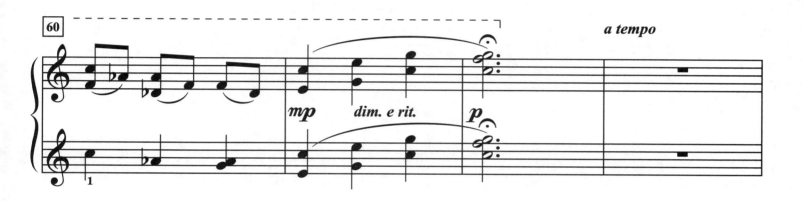

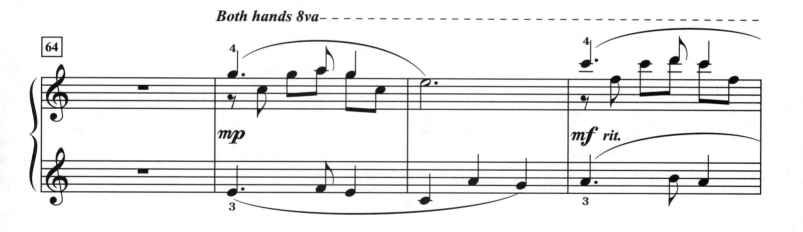

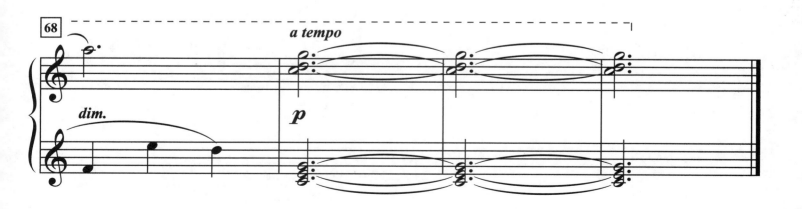

Joy to the World

SECONDO

George Frideric Handel
Arr. Robert D. Vandall

Joy to the World

PRIMO

George Frideric Handel
Arr. Robert D. Vandall

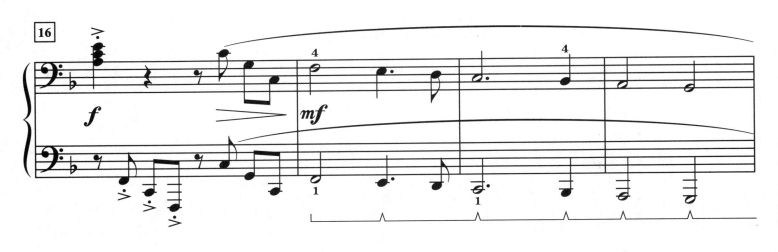

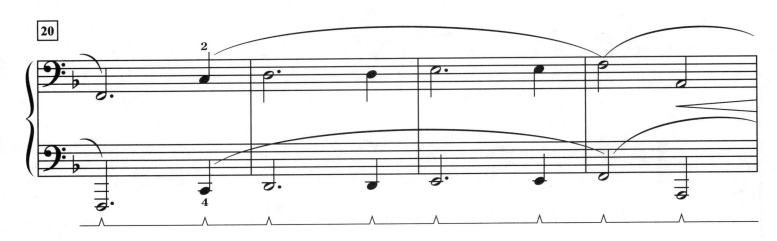

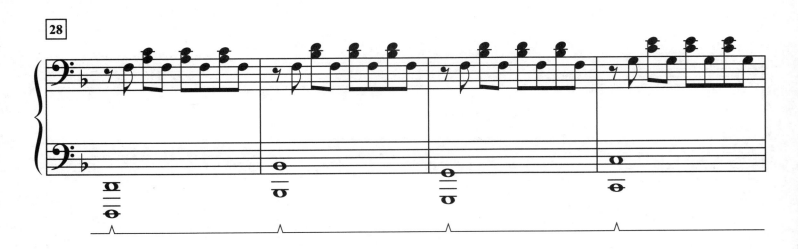

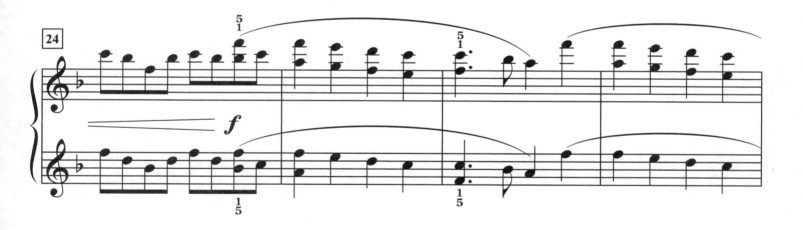

40

SECONDO

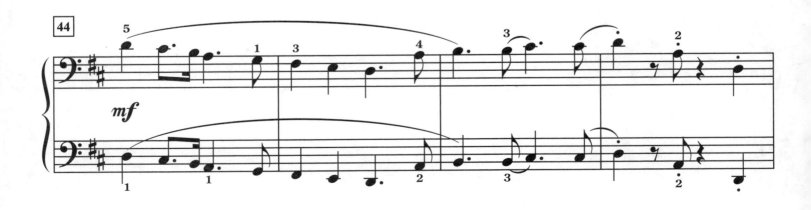

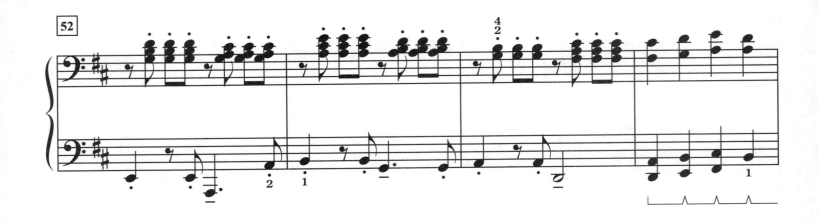

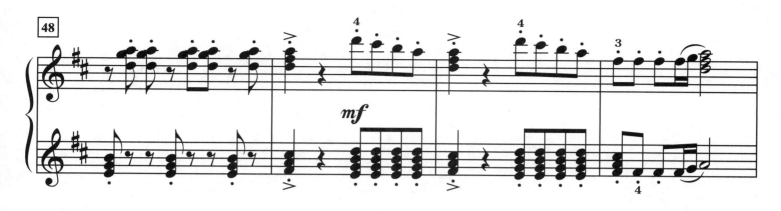

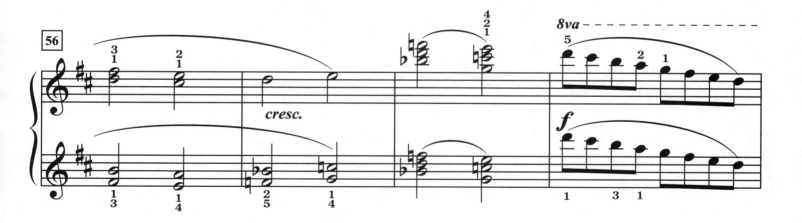

Believe

(from *The Polar Express*)

SECONDO

Words and Music by
Alan Silvestri and Glen Ballard
Arr. Robert D. Vandall

Believe

(from *The Polar Express*)

PRIMO

Words and Music by
Alan Silvestri and Glen Ballard
Arr. Robert D. Vandall

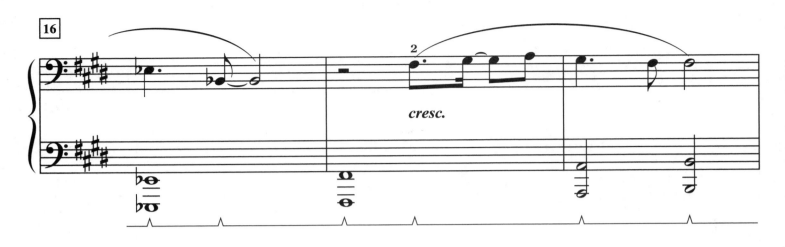

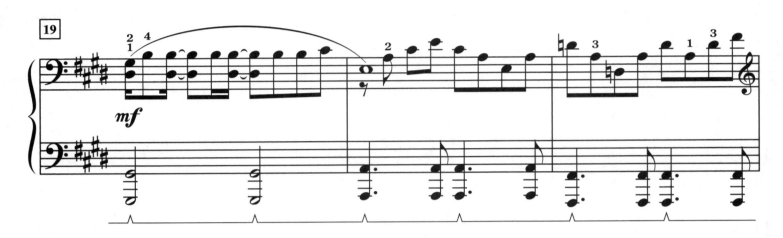

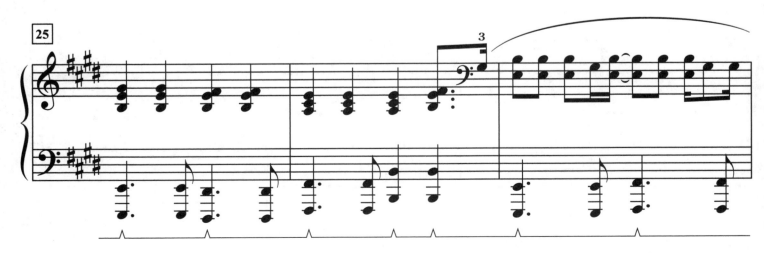

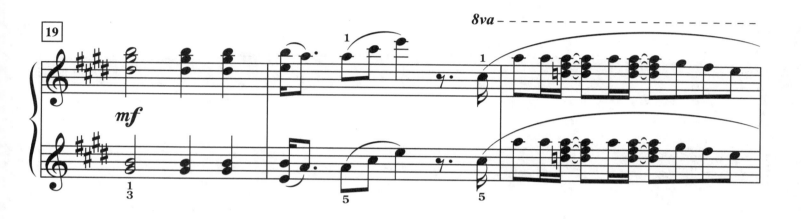

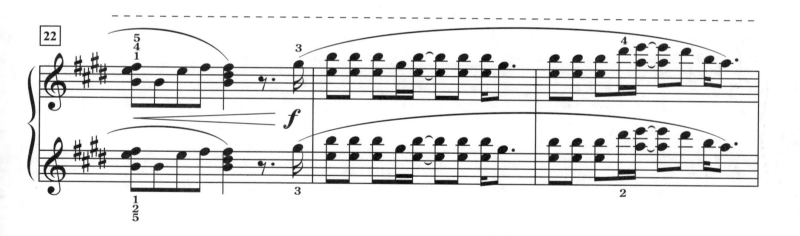

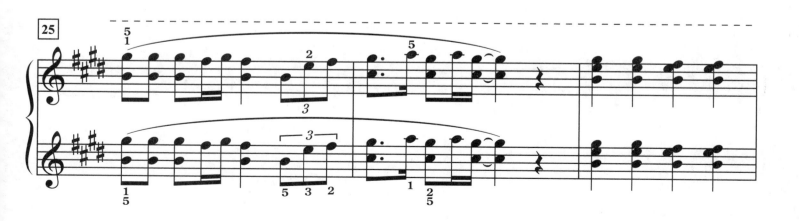

SECONDO

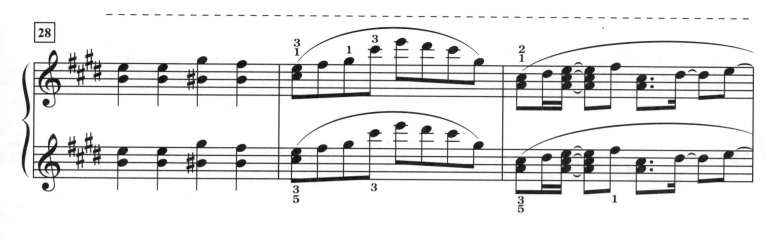

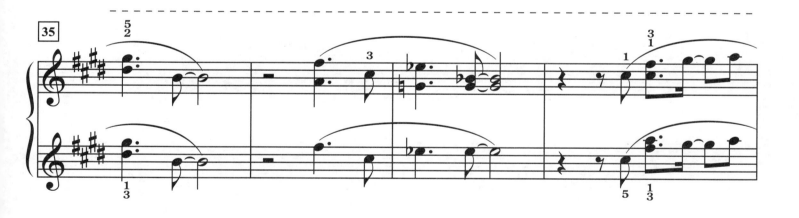

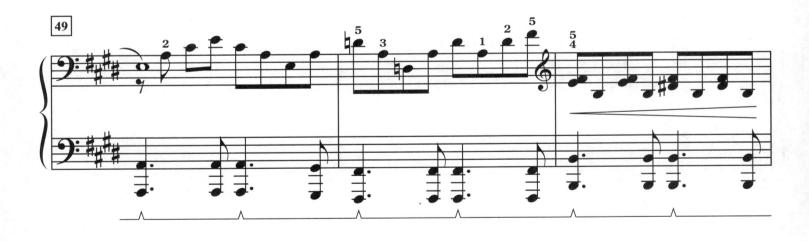
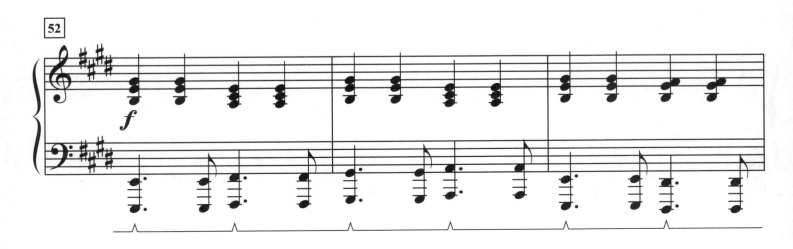

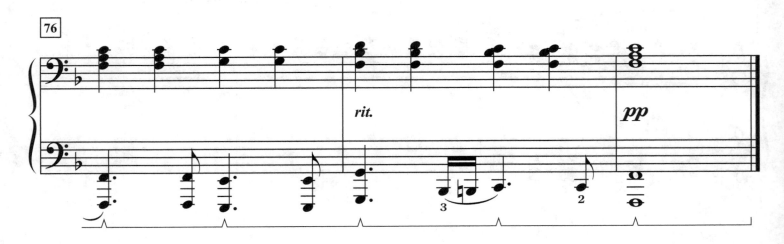